There's no age limit to being a Girl Warrior. She doesn't look a particular way. She comes in all ages, sizes, shapes, colors. She's out there. And inside every girl who enters the world. She's the face of hope at the bottom of Pandora's Box.

★ PRODUCTIONS ★

ISBN 978-1-09831-927-4

Girlwarriorproductions.com

Cover and interior design by Carisse Tam,
H2 Accelerator

Posts
From The
High Wire

Becoming a Girl Warrior.

I'm a warrior. It's taken me decades to accept this notion. But I now know it to be true. How could I have been otherwise? I was raised by one of the best warriors God ever created. Ma, my Warrior Queen. The courageous one. The small package containing a fierce and valiant spirit. My inspiration. Teacher. Leader. The one I will follow into the dark.

I have raised two glorious Girl Warriors. They too inspire me. Every day and in every way. They stand tall. And walk with their own swagger. Speak their truth. They challenge. Question. Test. They are noble. I have a grand daughter who is a young Girl Warrior. Already fiercely independent. A mind of her own. An adventurer off to see the world. No holding her back. Then there's my bonus Girl Warrior. My daughter-in-law. The one who captured my son's attention and the hearts of his entire family. Another small package containing a wondrous, magical, audacious soul.

These extraordinary Girl Warriors, along with an army of others, have taught me much over the years. They've helped me unearth my Girl Warrior. To not be afraid of her magical powers. To celebrate. Honor. Appreciate. And applaud.

There's no age limit to being a Girl Warrior. She doesn't look a particular way. She comes in all ages, sizes, shapes, colors. She's out there. And inside every girl who enters the world. She's the face of hope at the bottom of Pandora's Box.

This book is dedicated to her.

Be Real.

Be real Girl Warrior. Authentically you. Be the girl you are when you're alone in your room. Because that girl, that brilliant bold beautiful girl, is simply the best there is. No one else quite like her. Powerful and pure magic.

She's the spontaneous girl who sings into her hairbrush. Or dances like a wild one. The girl who jumps on her bed with crazy abandon. And cries in her mirror so bad the mascara runs like black rivers down her cheeks. A girl who curses at the ceiling and vows to never speak again. The one who drops to her knees and prays that someone or something is listening.

Be the girl, who not only hears the music, but also makes the music. The girl who doesn't just march to the beat of her own drum but runs, leaps and flies. She's the leader of the band. Not the groupie.

Go ahead girl. Open the door to your room. Let the rest of the world see this strong, courageous, and one hundred percent genuine, Girl Warrior.

Stare Down Your Fears.

Stare down your fears Girl Warrior. Look them straight in the eyes. Laugh at them. Call their bluff. Walk right through them. Don't go around. Don't avoid. Face them head-on. Take a deep breath. Or a hundred breaths.

Make your move. And keep moving. Shaky legs, a racing heart, lump in the throat or dry mouth are just the silly antics of fear. Not real. Feel the fear and do it anyway. Find your brave heart and take it into battle. Give yourself a hug, girl.

Then go out and kick some ass.

Get a Kick Out of Life.

Get a kick out of life Girl Warrior. Have fun. Find things that amuse and delight you. Not just once in a while. But every single day.

Don't put it off for the weekend. For that vacation you may not take. Or some time in the future when all the stars line up perfectly. Don't wait for when you've got it made in the shade to let your hair down and let loose. Do it now.

Hoot and holler. Find your zippity doo dah. Dance your ass off. Make a joyful sound. Cause a ruckus. Bang on your drum all day. Laugh your guts out. Until you cry. Embrace happiness. Enjoy the people you're with right this very second, girl.

Let them see your playful radiant blithe heart.

Let in the Love.

Open your heart wide and let in the love. Go where your heart leads you. And don't run from its softness. Let it be tender. Kind. Compassionate. Gentle. Extend your hand to another and grab on tight. Then let go.

Therein lies your strength Girl Warrior.

Love again. Then again. And again. You don't have to get it right. Or perfect. Just let love come naturally. Accept that sometimes it will hurt. Don't let this frighten you. Don't push it away. Or turn your back. Don't give up on it. Most importantly, learn to recognize love when it comes your way. It doesn't always come gift wrapped. Sometimes it comes in a brown paper bag.

Your power to love will always be your secret weapon Girl Warrior.

Find Your Tribe.

Find your tribe. Your pack. Your posse. Your band of sisters and brothers. Surround yourself with people you trust, respect and enjoy. You don't have to always agree. You don't even have to always get along. Because when you're with your tribe you can safely debate or differ and still land together.

Nothing will break your bond Girl Warrior.

These are your faithful ones. Loyal. Steadfast. And true. The ones you can count on, who will be there for you, even when they're miles away. And they'll be with you, if not in person, then virtually. They'll be by your side. Shoulder to shoulder. They've got you.

And girl, these are the ones who will hold your hair back while you barf.

Find Your Passions.

Follow your passions Girl Warrior. Therein lies your love affair with life. Be curious. Channel your inner Curious George. Do things that you love to do. Be enthusiastic. Keen. Overflowing with zeal, zest and gusto. Embrace new ideas and ways of doing the things you already know. Be creative. Imaginative.

Take the magical mystery tour. Expand. Grow. Cultivate. Hone. Set your heart on fire. Grab a handful. Then another. And another. Gush about the things you love. Take risks. Embrace the failures on the way to your successes. Learn and get on with it.

Dive in with your whole heart, girl.

Be Generous.

Be generous. In every way. With everything and everybody. Don't be stingy. Don't withhold. Don't hang onto
things. Never covet. Give of what you have. What you
know. Give a little. Or give a lot. But give.

And forgive. For that is the ultimate gift. To others.
To yourself.

Give it all away without hesitation. And watch it all
come back in miraculous ways. Go out there and be
someone's blessing. You will be blessed in return.

It's the way of the Girl Warrior.

Be Honest.

Be honest. Speak up. Speak out. Speak your truth.
Express yourself. Whatever that means to you. However that looks. Tell it like it is. Or how you wish it was.
Be bold. Audacious in your speech. Intrepid with your
message.

But don't use your words to slaughter, Girl Warrior.

Lift not lower. Use your words to empower. Elucidate.
Illuminate. Exalt. Demystify. Enlighten. Make it good.
So damn good they'll be coming back for more of what
you've got to say.

But most importantly, take ownership of what comes
out of your mouth, girl.

Take Risks.

Take risks. Big ones. Small ones. The kind only you know you're taking. This is your deal. Go out on a limb. Get rid of the safety net. Free fall. Hang ten. Step out. And step off. Close your eyes and let go.

Fall in love with uncertainty Girl Warrior. Welcome unpredictability. Embrace the random unexpected things with open arms and wide-eyed wonder.

Don't play it safe. Just play it with everything you've got. Let the cards land where they will. And then play those too. Put yourself out there even when you'd rather hide under a rug. Don't have second thoughts. Or third.

Don't let anything or anyone sabotage your efforts. Squash your dreams. Take away your power. Don't doubt yourself. Not even for one second.

Take a chance. Venture forth. Give it your best shot. Something mind-blowing will happen when you do, girl.

Defend and Stand Up for Something.

Defend and stand up for something. That's what true Girl Warriors do. Don't stand on the sidelines. Believe in something.

If you haven't got a cause. Find one. The mission is personal. And it's critical. Don't worry if you're the only one fighting for it. That's not the point. If it's meaningful to you, then get behind it. Breathe life into it in a way only you can.

While you're standing up for something, avoid putting someone else down. No matter how much you disagree. Cheap shots are easy and beneath you. Defend their right to have their own beliefs. Don't kick or trample on the weak. Reach out and extend a helping hand.

Girl, invite them to stand with you.

Be in the Moment.

Be in the Moment. Be present. Fully engaged. Right here. Right now. Don't waste one single solitary second being anywhere else than where you are at this very instant. For this is all you truly have.

The past is done, girl. You can love what once was but don't live there. Don't fret over the things you regret. Or worry about all those woulda coulda shoulda things either. They have nothing to do with the way things are today.

The future is out there. Somewhere. But it is not yet yours. It's merely part of the exquisite possibilities. Not the beautiful bird already in your hand. This isn't to say you shouldn't have dreams. Or plans. And schemes.

Goals and aspirations are worthwhile. And may one day lead to your success. But if you spend all your days living in tomorrow and squander this precious hour, then in the end you have lost the greatest gift of all.

Awaken all your senses to "the now" Girl Warrior. And just be.

Believe in Something Bigger than Yourself.

Believe in something bigger than yourself Girl Warrior. Know that you are connected to every living thing in this marvelous Universe. That's a huge and daunting thought. So take it in. Fully. Breathe life into it. Wrap your loving arms around this notion until it seeps into your DNA and fills every cell. Clog your pores with this concept.

Figure out your place in the grander scheme of things. The beautiful, elegant, ingenious, creative, intelligent and precisely perfect design that dwells deep inside your soul. And that of every single being and creature that ever was. And ever will be. Imagine that.

Honor this exquisite essence.

Whether you call it God or Gitchi Manitou, Divine Intelligence or Great Spirit, Energy or Electricity, Jesus or Jane, it matters not. What really matters is the knowledge that you are a part of it. You are an essential drop of water in the great big sea. A twinkle in the starry night. A slice of light in the infinite sky. Your presence is requested. Here and now. For eternity.

And girl, you are never alone.

Take Good Care of Yourself.

Take good care of yourself. Do whatever it takes to be physically healthy. All the days of your life. Do it for yourself. And for all the people who love you. Be active in every arena of your life.

Find the thing that moves you, girl. Go to the gym. Take a fitness class. Play a sport. Be part of the team. Or go it alone. Do the Sun Salutation every morning in the tranquility of your bedroom. Walk the dog after supper. Chase the cat around the yard. Climb a mountain. Run down the hill. Swim circles around the competition. Pole dance. Or plié at the barre. Go fly a kite. Or paddle a canoe.

Whatever floats your boat. Makes you feel alive and well in your skin. You don't have to master it. You just have to do it.

Get off the couch, away from the table, or out of the bed. That's half the battle. You need to be strong Girl Warrior. Fit as a fiddle and in fighting form.

Ready for anything.

Have Impeccable Manners.

Have impeccable manners. There is no excuse for rudeness. Anywhere. Anytime. Treat everyone respectfully and politely. Please and thank you go a long way.

Be courteous and considerate at all times. Especially in those situations when you're on the receiving end of someone else's bad form. Take the high road. Always. Pump up the volume on your pleasantness. And you will see how disarming it can be. It's powerful stuff.

Remember the Golden Rule. Carry it around in your hip pocket. And pull it out whenever you need a little reminder. Treat others the way you would like to be treated Girl Warrior.

It's that simple.

Never Stop Learning.

Never stop learning. Your education doesn't end with the cap and gown. Or the walk across the stage to collect your diploma. Truth is, it's just beginning.

26   Be infinitely inquisitive, interested and intrigued by everything and everyone. Be eager to know and understand. Look under rocks. Check out every leaf and blade of grass. Peek behind curtains. Peer into windows. Pry open doors. Poke around. Pursue relentlessly the 'who, what, where and why' of life. Plant seeds of greatness. And pick the brains of the brightest.

Be a big thinker.

Grow your mind every day. Cultivate your intellect. Expand your knowledge. Enrich your life with new experiences. Seek wisdom in the nests of the sagacious old birds. Hunt tenaciously for truth. Let your mind wander. And wonder. Live life fully and may it be your finest teacher.

Read voraciously. Write prodigiously. Listen judiciously. Observe keenly. Ask questions. Be a perennial student Girl Warrior.

Until you draw your final breath.

Grow Your Compassion Muscle.

Grow your compassion muscle. Be kind. Make this your 'go to' virtue in every situation. Ask yourself, if I say this or do that, what effect will it have? Not just on others, but on yourself. What's the trickle-down effect? The pebble skipping across the water? The ripple in the still pond? The echo across the canyon?

How you treat others matters. Not just in small or imperceptible ways either, but also the universal, the colossal, and the cosmic. For we are not islands. We are all connected so it is imperative that you cause no harm. Instead foster big-heartedness and benevolence.

Imagine yourself in someone else's shoes. Walk a mile in their moccasins or mukluks or Manolos. Seek understanding. Express genuine concern. Cultivate a magnanimous spirit. Even towards those who seem impossible to love or unworthy. Herein lies your greatest workout. Exercise your tenderness and tolerance.

Compassion and loving-kindness are the heart and soul's great healers. Know this Girl Warrior and you will always be well.

Extend Grace.

Extend grace. Especially if you want to receive it. Know that there may come a day when you'll want nothing more than this merciful gift from another.

We all make mistakes, for we are only human after all. First and foremost, be forgiving when someone makes a mistake. Accept that things often go awry. Run amok. Go off the rails. Turn out all wrong with disappointing results.

Shit happens Girl Warrior. Understand that unfortunate things occur, even with the best intentions and the most valiant efforts. Resist the urge to point fingers, assign blame or throw someone under the bus. This doesn't accomplish anything. Nor does it move the conversation in the direction it needs to go.

And girl, always give what you want to get.

Be Someone's Blessing Today.

Be someone's blessing today Girl Warrior. A glorious Godsend. Wonderful windfall. Lucky penny. Look for all the ways you can make someone else's life easier or more meaningful. Lighten their load. Lift their spirits. Ease their burdens. Dry their tears. Make someone's day.

Listen attentively. And look deep into their eyes. Extend a helping hand. Wrap your arms around the one in need of a hug. Calm the trembling shoulders. Hold the door open. Be of service. Give someone a leg up. Or save their bacon. Do favors and expect nothing in return.

Be someone who can be counted on, trusted, relied upon, and the wind beneath the wings. Most importantly, just be there when needed.

This is the perfect paradox. Bless and be blessed.

Hang Out
in Nature.

Hang out in nature. Get to know the wonder and magic of the great outdoors. It's a vast and infinite playground. And it's all yours to explore Girl Warrior.

32 No matter where you are. Regardless of how busy you think you are. Stop and make time. Leave. Get outside. Every day. You don't have to go far. Nor does it have to be a convoluted affair. Take a ten-minute walk around the block or down a dirt road. Go to your thinking place by the sea, lake, ocean or stream. Dig your toes in the desert sand. Run barefoot or strap on snowshoes. Soar with the eagles or swim with the turtles. Go into the woods or climb that mountain.

Commune with Mother Earth.

She lives everywhere. Even in the most crowded cities. A tree grows in Brooklyn. A bird sings in Singapore.

Flowers bloom in Boston. The point is, the world is a beautiful, majestic, awe-inspiring place. And it beckons.

Heed the call, girl.

*Be in the Moment.
Be present. Fully
engaged. Right here.
Right now. For this
is all you truly have.*

Eat Well and Wise.

Eat well and wise Girl Warrior. Learn how to cook for yourself and the ones you love. Keep it simple. Get fresh with food. Know its origins. Get the back-story on your fruits and veggies. Do your homework. Read labels. Eat things of the earth and near to their natural state. Be creative in the kitchen. Experiment. Get colorful and crazy. Explore what titillates and tantalizes your taste buds. Make it pretty.

You don't have to be a Food Fanatic either. Nor a Nutrition Nazi. Make 'everything in moderation' your mantra. Think balance. Nurture your body and your spirit. Apply the 80/20 Rule. 80% healthy and 20% not-so-much. Enjoy your guilty pleasures and sweet indulgences without regret or ruefulness. Whet your appetite fully. Savor it all. Go for the gusto.

And eat like your life depends on it girl.

Create The Soundtrack of Your Life.

Create the soundtrack for your life. You've got the music in you. Let it out. Wherever. Whenever. Don't be shy. Or embarrassed. Don't listen to your inner judge. The one that says you're tone deaf. Can't carry a tune. Have no talent. It's not about that. It's about joy and wild abandon. Harmony in hard places.

It's one of the best things you can do for your body, mind and spirit. So get musical. From your bobbing head to your tapping toes. Put a song in your heart. Let it rest easy in your soul. And flow through your veins like Tupelo Honey.

Pick up a guitar. Shake a tambourine. Beat a bongo drum. Stomp your feet. Snap your fingers. Clap your hands. Sing in the shower. Or in your truck. Join a choir. Or form a band.

You don't have to be a virtuoso. You don't even have to be any good. In fact, you can be terrifically terrible. There are far worse things Girl Warrior.

Like dying with the music still locked inside you.

Be Still.

Be still. Sit quietly. Spend time alone gazing inward. It's a breathtaking sight. Take a moment every day for introspection. Meditate. Pray. Twenty minutes in the solitude of your room is all you need to be transformed. It will change your mind. And alter your life.

Unplug. Turn everything off. Including the lights but especially all your digital devices. No distractions. No diversions. No disturbances.

Let nothing come between you and your inner self. This is your time to just be. And get in touch with who you really are Girl Warrior. Deep down in your core.

Shut out the noise and the clatter. Sink into the silence. It is here that you will find peace. Surrender to serenity. It's as natural as breathing. In. Out. In. Out.

Let the calm beautiful you emerge, girl. Like a butterfly from the chrysalis.

Hang Around with Animals.

Hang around with animals. It's next to impossible to be in a foul mood when you do Girl Warrior. They have an infinite capacity to lift the spirits of their human friends. You'll be happier in their furry or feathery company. Your beaming joyous face is proof positive.

Pet a dog when you're anxious and within minutes you'll be relaxed. Watch a cat chase a light beam around the room and you'll find yourself giggling hysterically. Cuddle a bunny and you'll know instantly why good things come in small packages. Sit in front of a fish tank for ten minutes and without effort you'll be meditating. Listen to the birds sing and you'll know what real communication is all about. Get on the back of a horse and you'll understand the true meaning of balance and strength.

If you're feeling blue, they'll brighten your day. If you're lonely, they'll be there. They'll teach you things about loyalty, faithfulness, dedication, steadfastness, resilience, trust, courage and bravery.

And most importantly, about unconditional love.

Take Care of
Your Habitat.

Take care of your habitat Girl Warrior. It's the only real home you've got. And right now it's fragile. Vulnerable. Compromised. And in a very tenuous state, hanging on by a thin perilous thread. Which means so are you and everyone you love, everything you hold dear, and everything that matters to you.

The truth, the very inconvenient truth of Al Gore, is we created this situation. It's our mess and we have to get ourselves out of it. Quite simply we have to clean it up. Now.

It's an intimidating thought, a daunting task, a formidable challenge, and an enormous responsibility. But you're a Girl Warrior and you were born to take this on. Not alone, but with your Tribe of fierce, tenacious, unshakeable sisters and brothers who understand fully what's at stake. And the urgency with which you need to take action and respond to the brokenhearted cry of the land you walk on, the air you breathe, the water you consume, the energy and natural resources that sustain you, the mighty weeping environment that has given you life.

There is no time to waste. Or squander recklessly. You can no longer languish in unmindful, uninformed, unconscious, nescient blind bliss, pretend or make-believe. The days of your innocence are over. You have been woken up and you cannot go back. Ever.

You can still chase the beautiful rainbows, the ephemeral butterflies and the buzzing bees. But first girl, you have to save them.

Dress the Part.

Dress the part. Every Girl Warrior should have a costume. Something that is uniquely her. At first blush, it might look just like someone else's. Don't be fooled. No two Girl Warriors wear their costumes in the same way. This is your personal power suit. Put it on.

Strut your stuff, girl.

Don't apologize for the cut, color or condition. Walk. Run. Skip to my Lou. Black leather jacket. Frilly blouse. Skinny jeans. Mini skirt. Floor length gown. A sundress blooming with flowers. Floppy hat. Or fascinator. A pinstriped suit. Kick-ass boots. Red stiletto shoes.

It's not about fashion.

It's about expression. Wearing the inside out. It's about attitude. Character. Originality. You are a rare bird Girl Warrior. Know this.

So put on your cape. And fly.

Leave the Herd.

Sometimes you have to leave the herd Girl Warrior. Pull away from the pack. And step out on your own. Fly solo. Go it alone. Take on the world single-handedly and forge a path that only you can walk.

This can be a frightening proposition. Terrifying. The mere thought may paralyze you. But don't let it. Dig down deep into your Girl Warrior heart. Let it reveal all the reasons why you need to take this solitary journey. For in this sacred and sincere examination of all the light and dark places of your marrow you will discover that this is the only way you can get to the next step. This is what you need to do before you can fly.

And fly you must.

On this soul search pilgrimage you will discover some very deep truths about who you are and what you are made of. You will learn about the full depth and breadth and height of your character, rectitude, integrity, honor, principles, virtues and pure sweet goodness.

There is so much goodness.

Walk bravely and boldly through the refiner's fire Girl Warrior. And know that your Tribe is not only waiting for your glorious and triumphant return, but that they have been there with you every step of the way. They were in the wind and rain and dust and dirt. In the forests and the mountains and seas and deserts. In the cities and villages and small towns and whistle-stops. Their abiding spirits were with you in the sunshine and in the sorrow, in the wilderness of your purpose and the wanderlust of your desires.

And when you are done girl, they will be there cheering while you don your cape.

Start Over.

It's never too late to start over. To press the refresh button. Begin anew. Hit reset, reboot or recharge. Give yourself a second chance. Or third, fourth, tenth, hundred times a hundred.

And see what happens.

No matter where or what you've been or done or said or not said up until this very moment, matters not. Really, truly, completely absorb this. Believe it. Not just with your mind but with your heart. In fact, let your heart take the lead with this particular endeavor. For your heart's ancient omnipresent wisdom will guide you every step of the way. It will not fail you.

So fear not.

Then, remember the innocence, the wonder and pure

gorgeousness of your Little Girl Warrior. Remember her? She's there now and always has been. Go back to her. Wrap your loving arms around her. Have a heart to heart. Take her by the hand. Renew your acquaintance with this precious person. The young Girl Warrior, who wore the cape and armed with wide-eyed wonder and a great big unstoppable imagination, believed she could be anyone, do anything, go anywhere. Conquer the world in her rare and one-of-a-kind fashion. She was radiant Starshine. And she is still with you.

Girl Warrior, wipe the slate clean and go out and reinvent yourself today in a way that would make Little Girl Warrior proud. So proud.

Don't Put Your Life on Hold.

Don't put your life on hold. For any reason. The cliché that life is not a dress rehearsal bears truth here. This is it. It's all you've got. Your one shot. Press pause if you must. But the odds are, and the sad truth is, time is ticking and waits for no one. Not even Girl Warriors.

All those things you want to do. All your best-laid plans, sunny afternoon daydreams, earnest heartfelt intentions, picturesque vision boards and bulls-eye targets are a nice start. But that's all they are. A place to begin. A clarification process. The un-muddying exercise. Allowing the puddle to settle so you can see clearly.

The cautionary tale: don't get stuck here. For if you linger too long in this complacent stage of artificial activity, engaging in all those time-wasting diversions instead of pursuing the real things that add truth and meaning to your life, you'll turn around one day and wonder what happened. You'll ask yourself one of the most tragic personal questions there is, "How did this happen?"

So don't procrastinate, girl. Get off your legendary ass. Knock it off. And get on with it. Live your best life. Now.

Don't Live in a Bubble.

Don't live your life in a bubble Girl Warrior. Because when you do you rob yourself of the beautiful richness, texture and abundance outside your safe little cocoon. Yes, there are complications and conflicts, tests and trials, stumbling blocks and drawbacks, chaos and confusion. All kinds of messiness and tangled yuck. And there are people. Other people. And not all of them think like you or the ones in your front row, front room, or front line.

Don't shut down. And more importantly don't shut others down.

Girl Warrior, it's critical, now more than ever, to listen to others. Even if they have opposing points of view. Even if they have different opinions. Even if they have different political affiliations. Even if they worship at a different house. Even if they are from a different culture. Even if their skin is a different color. Even if their gender identity conflicts with your ideology. And yes even if their love for another is beyond your comprehension.

Sit amongst those with different belief systems Girl Warrior. Uncross your arms. Remove the blinders from your eyes. Hold your tongue. Unclench your jaw and fists. Open the window of your mind and the ears of your heart. Prepare yourself for receptivity so you can explore the art of the possible. You might learn something. Not just about them but about yourself.

The goal is understanding and appreciation for the intentions of others. You don't have to agree but you must disagree respectfully. Strive to honor where another is coming from—where their journey began and what lead them to this space. Resist the temptation to judge, to cast aspersions, vilify or condemn. Instead work towards seeing the world through their lens, from their perspective and vantage point. Again, you don't have to agree or embrace it. But for your own sake, you should allow yourself to hear it. Only then can you make an honest assessment.

To do this, girl you may have to grow a thicker skin, a broader backbone and stiffer spine. You're not a baby in pampers who needs coddling. You've got guts and fortitude. More than you know. Life isn't always a bed of roses. And you aren't a delicate flower. You are also wise enough to know the difference between hate speech and freedom of expression. This isn't about hate but the extension of love and kindness to all humans.

Situations aren't blatantly and simplistically black and white Girl Warrior. Neither are humans. If you are willing to listen, with an open mind and heart, you just might find that the things you have in common far outweigh the differences.

Get Back Up.

Get back up Girl Warrior. When you get knocked down.
Thrown to the ground or thrown for a loop. When life
tosses you a curve ball or chucks you to the curb, don't
take it lying down. Don't give in. Don't give up. Get up.
And then get on with it.

Shit happens. That's the truth. It's also the truth that it
happens to everybody. The thing is, and this is the really
hard part to digest, it's appallingly indiscriminate. It
doesn't care if you are smart or dumb, rich or poor, nice
or naughty, fit or fat, kind or cruel, good or bad, tall or
short, religious or atheist, vegan or carnivore, pretty or
not so much. It simply does not care. Sooner or later
bad juju is going to come blowing your way. So know
that. And then get on with it.

It's not the bad luck or the bad juju. It's not about getting
knocked down or knocked out or knocked up. And it's

not even necessarily about poor little old you. It's really not that personal. Or all that malevolent, malicious or maleficent. Much of the time, if you stare this bugaboo in the face, you realize it's not that purposeful or intentional. It's often quite random, arbitrary and arrantly benign. Just something or someone you open-handedly gave your power to. Take it back. And get on with it.

So if it isn't about any of that stuff, then what is it about?

It's about what you do when shit happens. It's about how you react. And act. It's about your perception. And reception. It's about your attitude. And gratitude. It's about your viewpoint. And outlook. It's about your response. And repercussions. It's about your recovery. And resurgence. It's about your upturn. And comeback.

And most importantly, it's about what you do after the knockout, after the shit-kicking. And that, girl is entirely up to you. It's your call.

Walk the high wire without a safety net. And learn to love it.

Embrace Your Inner Weirdo.

Go beyond your IQ Girl Warrior and embrace your IW. Your Inner Weirdo is the most glorious and incomparable thing about you. The best. The thing that makes you uniquely you. Beautifully unorthodox. Boldly unconventional. Brilliantly rare. And yes, sometimes even odd.

Oddly extraordinary. Oddly surprising. Oddly awe-inspiring. And most importantly, oddly original. There's no one else like you in the whole wide world. Wow to that girl.

Let your gorgeous IW out of the box. Set her free.

But first, you must break through the barriers of fear, insecurity and doubt. None of these are real. They merely dwell in the dark side of your big imagination and are fabricated to keep you small and contained. Posers, Phonies and Pretenders. Kick them aside, step right through and march on. Then put your imagination, and all the gifts your IW brings to the table, to better use.

Your IW will bring a fresh perspective to the way you interact and interface with all the people, places and things in your cosmos. Everything changes when you emancipate your IW. New insights. Deeper understanding. Increased clarity. Profound appreciation. Greater gratitude.

More love. More laughter. More joy. More silliness. More spontaneity. More creativity.

More of all the things. From the ridiculous to the sublime. Your IW has a knack for bringing out "the more." The everyday is transformed, the common is inspired, the ordinary becomes extraordinary.

Your IW has the power to open your eyes so wide that the world around you is suddenly and profoundly illuminated, hopeful, promising and acutely reassuring.

Girl Warrior, you have not only found your place on Earth, you have found your people. Let that settle in for a moment. These are your courageous and crazy-sweet tribe of weirdoes who have opened their arms and hearts with acceptance, unconditional love and grace.

And remember, they may be weirdoes but they are your weirdoes. Wow and wow to that girl.

Read Books.

Read books Girl Warrior. Fall in love with this beautiful skill that you learned in elementary school. Make reading a daily lifelong habit, a sacred ritual and part of your DNA. Embrace and covet this practice so fiercely that not reading feels abnormal, wrong, off-kilter, not yourself.

If you make reading books part of your routine, like brushing your teeth, it will serve you so well all the days of your life. It's a game-changer. Guaranteed. That is the noble and profound power of books. They will be amongst your wisest teachers and hold the key to your enlightenment in every aspect of your humanity. Books, and a good mentor, will take you far and wide and deep and high.

Books will also take you places you may never get to experience otherwise. Not just in the physical world but in the spiritual, intellectual and emotional realms as well. Books will enable you to travel in time. Back to the pre-historic and ahead to the fantastical future. Adventures abound in the pages of a good book, well beyond the boundaries and limitations of your logical mind. Oh, the places you'll go! (Dr. Seuss)

Books will grow your creativity and inventiveness, expand your consciousness and touch your heart. They'll make you cry out all the tears, laugh uncontrollably until you pee your pants, scare the shit out of you, make you face unbearable truths, fall head-over-heels in love, and allow you to fly so high you'll understand why birds sing. Your intellectual curiosity will not only be stimulated but satisfied. You'll be an enduring Curious George. The really big payoff with all of this book reading is you'll be continuously challenged and inspired by ideas, concepts, images, theories, opinions, philosophies, people, places and all things Seussian.

So Girl Warrior head to your nearest library or bookstore —online, around the corner, downtown or in the mall— and begin this very important life-altering practice.

Then do the following: hold the book in your hands, smell its inky newness or mustiness if it's a used treasure; run your fingers along the spine and over the cover; touch the dog-eared pages for this means it's well-read, well-shared and well-loved by many other book-lovers just like you; and above all, breathe in all the information, knowledge and wisdom the book possesses, and honor it by bringing it home.

And then experiment with these: curl up on the sofa on a snowy afternoon with a good mystery thriller. Bring a summer bestseller to the beach. Luxuriate in the tub with a glass of wine and an inspiring biography. Take your juicy novel to bed with you. And by the way, public transit takes on a whole new meaning when you learn something new on your commute. Join a book club or start one. Go to an author reading and bask in the sound of their voice. It's like they are reading a bedtime story just for you. It doesn't get much better than that for a book lover.

Girl Warrior, talk about the books you've read. Inspire others to read books too. Share your joy of reading, of the written word, of the brilliance of storytelling, and of the mystery and music of language. It is such a privilege to be able to read books. Just ask someone who can't or someone who has been denied access.

Say I Love You to Yourself.

Self-care is more than getting pedicures, facials, eyebrow waxes or shiatsu massages Girl Warrior. That's only part of the picture. Treating yourself to a "me day" can include all the nurturing things that we do for our external selves, the outside part that we present to the world every day. There's nothing wrong with showing off our pretty.

Wanting our Earth Suit to look and feel its best isn't about vanity. It's about confidence and self-assurance. Feeling good in our own skin. And expressing it outwardly.

Gifting yourself the spa treatment is an act of loving kindness towards your body. If a spa isn't available to you then turn your home into one for a day. Either way, go ahead pamper yourself. Take a break from all the noise and distraction of the outside world. Indulge in all the activities that make your body feel honored and cared for. Send it the message that it is important, a priority. This is your day. Take it.

Light aromatherapy candles. Unwind in a skin-nourishing bubble bath. Relax with a good book or your favorite magazine. Listen to soothing music or rock 'n roll if that's what soothes you. Do some gentle yoga stretches. Prepare a simple, healthy meal. Eat chocolate. Drink your favorite herbal tea from the finest cup you own, the one reserved for special times. Like this. Watch a funny movie and laugh your guts out. Or a sad one and cry like a baby. Cuddle up with a furry friend. Do all these beautiful loving things Girl Warrior.

But don't stop there. For your body is only part of the picture.

Treating yourself to all these physical pleasures is the perfect way to set the stage for the really important stuff, the interior things that the world doesn't see. The metaphysical. The spiritual. Affairs of the heart. Mysteries of the mind. All the secret stuff locked or trapped inside you. Waiting.

Waiting on you Girl Warrior, to acknowledge, understand, appreciate and unleash the magnificence of the real you. The true blue you. But to do so, you must go deep. Deeper than skin, deeper than flesh and bones, deeper than blood, sweat and tears.

Just like there are many ways to care for your physical being, there are tools and things you can do to help unearth your true essence, the 'for real' one, the centered self, the everlasting being, the soul survivor.

Start with your breath. This is your connection to The Eternal and to every human walking the path of life, past and present. Breathe deep. Breathe slowly. Breathe intentionally. Then sit quietly. And turn your attention inwards. Focus on your breath, your life force. Be still. This is you meditating. Fear not. Let whatever comes to you—come. Observe. Learn. Let it go. Repeat.

When you emerge from this mystical practice of getting to know your true self, you'll probably feel more relaxed and closer to a state of peace and acceptance. But you may also feel a bit unsettled. This is your humanity talking. Respectfully honor it. Listen and record these thoughts and feelings in a journal. This is your book of revelations. It is here that you will learn the most about yourself—the things you desire, the things you fear, the things you hope for, the things you dream about and, most importantly, the things you love. For it is the things you love that make you real.

Then Girl Warrior say, "I love you" to the most influential person in your life. You.

Go From Me
to We.

Go from me to we Girl Warrior. Let that thought sink in for a moment. Now take your eyes and your mind and your thoughts off yourself and take a long hard look at the world around you. And ask yourself this question. Is

the relentless pursuit of self-improvement, self-growth, self-development, self-awareness, self-actualization and ultimately unconditional self-love really enough?

It is if this thing we call life was only about you. But the truth is, it isn't.

It's also about every other living soul and sentient being, both inside and outside, of your personal orbit. And we're all transients merely passing through this very particular time in evolution and history together. In essence we are all one great big colossal messy interesting complicated tangled perplexing challenging happy sad tragic joyous exceptional ordinary family. We are more alike than we are different. We are more homogeneous than we are disparate. And we need each other more than we often realize. Or care to admit.

We don't journey alone.

We don't rise or fall alone. We don't win or lose alone. We don't make it alone. We may die alone but we certainly don't live alone. And this is the truly beautiful part. This is the part where we get to grow outside of our own skin, beyond our own needs, wants and desires to become towering extraordinary spiritual beings having very human earthly experiences.

It is here that we get to be stellar and as vast as the night sky.

It is here that we get to express our extra-special-terrestrial nature. It is here that we get to extend our hand to another and humbly say, "I am here for you." Not as a perfect being, but as a willing one. Willing to do whatever it takes. Not just when it is easy or convenient but when it is so bloody hard and painful, when our nails are bitten raw and our knees are scraped to the bone, when the blood pours from our fragile hearts and our breath is squeezed and forsaken.

Here to help, as selflessly as humanly possible. Here to traverse from the other side of me to the divine place of we.

Starting today Girl Warrior, go out and do something that isn't about you.

Take a Leap of Faith.

Take a leap of faith. Especially in those pivotal moments that define the direction of your life, if not permanently, then for a colossal chunk of it. The make or break junctures. The pinpoint life-altering time that when you look back, you realize that, 'this was when it all started.'

Don't let that be the split-second that leaves you filled with an entire lifetime of regret.

Leaping can be scary.

Fear of failure or change or the unknown can be overwhelming and shake your confidence. Rock your foundation. Make the earth move under your feet so badly that you're knocked off-balance. Your equilibrium is quivering and quaking. That's what fear does. But fear is only false evidence appearing real. Not real. Just pretending. A schoolyard bully that you need to show who's the boss.

It's paramount that you don't allow doubt to seep into your thoughts, and then settle there like an ungracious houseguest. Not even for a bit. Take a deep breath and jump in. Headfirst. Feet-first. Nose-dive. Or ass-over-tea-kettle. It does not matter how, it just matters that you do.

If the faith in yourself is faltering, then jump with the faith that others have in you. Work with that. Seize their faith in you, embrace it and carry it in your heart and mind until you see what everyone else sees.

72 You've got this Girl Warrior. You can do it. You know you can.

Live Your Best Life.

Live your best life Girl Warrior. We hear it all the time. It's the new battle cry for the ages. But what does it actually mean? It's a loaded statement at best. Fraught with unspoken expectations, whispered doubts, onerous pressure and murky conjecture. Creating more tension than intention.

It invokes the comparison game. The implication is that what you are now isn't sufficient. Because the truth is, it's not just your best life you're chasing. No, that's not good enough. It's the better life. Not only better than the one you already possess, but also a life that is better than (fill in the blank). This knowledge breathes anxiety into every cell of your body. And robs you of the enjoyment of "what is." Your conscious self may not be aware. But Girl Warrior deep inside, where the wise woman dwells, you know the truth.

The evidence of best lives is everywhere. Facebook. Instagram. YouTube. Twitter. TV. Lifestyle websites. Self-improvement portals. Coaching pages. Tutorial videos. Webinars. Influencer blogs. Ted Talks. Instructing us on new and improved ways to think, feel, act, dress, eat, exercise and sleep. If you can dream it, you can stream it.

Best lives, are not only lived, but they are taught, bought, sought and caught.

The manifestation of our best lives is visually omnipresent. It's in our faces. You can't help but see it. Unless you're blind. The selfie smiles. Moody pensive gazes. Intelligent insightful expressions. Enlightened knowing eyes. Romantic poses. Goofy self-deprecating affectations. Hugs, kisses, laughter, tears. The emojis, clever words, inspiring quotes, beautiful photographs, animated gifs, boomerang and cool videos with equally cool soundtracks are all the ways we can express our best lives. Over and over and over.

It's so much work living our best lives. Keeping up is all so fucking exhausting.

How about this Girl Warrior? Relax. Take it easy. Loosen

up. Give yourself a break. And take it as it comes. Bit by bit. Live your own life—bad, good, better, best, or otherwise. The way you like it. Authentically. Honestly. With kindness, caring, compassion and generosity to others and yourself. No pressure. Just be. That's good enough.

Make It Awkward.

Make it awkward, especially in sticky difficult situations. Or during those times when your first inclination would be to cut your losses and walk away. Sometimes your first thought is the right thought. But there are times when you need to think again.

Stop, take a deep expansive breath and ask yourself this. How often have you let someone off the hook because you were too afraid?

Too afraid of confrontation. Too afraid of offending. Too afraid of hurting someone's feelings. Too afraid of speaking the truth. Too afraid of making a scene. Too afraid of embarrassing yourself. Too afraid of making someone angry. Too afraid of your own anger. Too afraid of what others might think. And ultimately, too afraid of losing someone's love or affection. Inevitably it all comes down to that.

Now stop again, take another deep expansive breath and ask yourself this. Is the answer yes?

If the answer is yes to even one of these questions, then it's time to take a risk. Time to take a stand. Time to gamble and put all your cards on the table. Time to do what you've always wanted to do in previous compromising circumstances. And if you're truly gutting the truth Girl Warrior, you've been here far too many times. Far too many times.

This is your triumphant do-over.

This is your opportunity to speak up and speak your truth. Once and for all. Succinctly. Emphatically. Definitively. You will need to summon all the courage you possess because making it awkward isn't easy. Walking away without making a peep is easy. Being a good girl who doesn't make waves is easy. Playing nice is easy.

But don't be a good girl in this situation.

Instead go for the squirm. Make it downright uncomfortable and bloody inconvenient. Remind yourself that you are a bold and brave Girl Warrior. And remember, you aren't taking this stand on your own. You have an entire Tribe of Girl Warriors behind you. Supporting and cheering you on.

So this time girl, make it awkward.

Get a Side Hustle.

Get yourself a side hustle Girl Warrior. A little some-thin' somethin' besides the thing you're doing right now. Especially if the thing that's going on right now isn't the thing. To be clear, this isn't a slam on the current thing. No aspersions cast and it's not what we're talking about here. It's about needing a little more somthin' in your something. More creativity. Intellectual challenge. Spir-itual satisfaction. Emotional fulfillment. And here's a really big thing. More money.

If you need a little more in your life Girl Warrior then it's time to earnestly look at other ways to bump up your something. Round out your life so that it's more amplified—fuller, richer, abundant, prosperous, satis-fying, complete, creative and categorically happier in every way. Design and define your best life, whatever that may be.

In an ideal world your perfect side hustle would be something you've always been longing to do, some secret passion you're aching to express or talent you want to bring out of hiding. But in reality your side hustle might be far more practical, a ways and means to earn extra money—to take a big trip, buy a house or a new car, pay off your debt or student loan. Whatever. It's equal parts blue-sky thinking and real-world pragmatism.

First you'll have to take a good look at your current situation to see what's missing, why it isn't enough and what you need. Ask yourself this: if the Queen Bee of All Girl Warriors appeared and waved a magic wand what would your quintessential life look like? Who would be in it? Where would you live? How would you spend your time? What are your priorities? What can you live with and without?

Then take inventory. Look at all the things you like to do outside of work, beyond the nine to five. Include everything in this assessment—from hobbies to volunteer work, the stuff you like to play whether it's sports or an instrument, what and where you love to eat, the kinds of people you like to hang out with, and where you like to go—both far and wide.

Then go hustle it up.

One cautionary note Girl Warrior. Your side hustle in no way gives you permission to be distracted, dismiss or slack off on your existing bread-and-butter job. Don't bite the hand that feeds you. Give it one hundred percent and then some. Or leave and make the side hustle, the thing.

Start Early.

Start your day early Girl Warrior. By doing so you will begin to activate your true genius. It is during these wee hours that you will find your purpose for the day. And for your life. You will explore new avenues and ways of thinking. You'll bring into the Light profound ways of being and a sage's understanding of your humanness. Gifts and talents will be unearthed during this time. The real you, that beautiful creature who first arrived here on Planet Earth, will be remembered, revived and rekindled. She will bring you inspiration and you will cherish her presence. You will meet her here at dawn.

Don't miss this opportunity to engage fully with her. This is a life-changing experience. One you get to do every day—if you choose to.

Get up before the rest of your household stirs. Give yourself at least an hour—and aim to grow it to two hours

—of alone time, quiet time, you time. This is your gift to yourself. Set the alarm an hour early if need be. Make that commitment to yourself. No hitting the snooze button. Get up.

Get up and before you do anything else, make your bed. If you don't sleep alone, make it after your partner rises. If your relationship policy has been 'last one up makes the bed' (which may mean it doesn't get made) then scrap that shit. Make the bed. This is about you, not them, and especially not about domestic rules or rivalries. It's about discipline, order, clarity, and doing something so very simple and basic, first. It's the magnificent metaphor for your day.

Because this time is dedicated soulfully and respectfully to you, no one else gets to determine how it looks or how it unfolds. Having said that, here are a few things to consider for making the most of your early-morning practice from a Girl Warrior with decades of daily pre-dawn sessions under her belt.

After you've made the bed, hydrate. Drink a glass of warmish water (with or without a splash of lemon). Find a warm quiet place free from all distractions, light a candle if you like, and take 10 to 20 minutes to meditate. Don't get bent out of shape about meditation either. The point is to simply sit quietly alone without any disturbances and diversions—human, animal or most importantly, digital. Don't worry about your mind wandering or your thoughts interrupting the flow. Just relax and let it be. This is your meditation. You define it so don't judge it. Just enjoy.

After meditation, spend time with your thoughts. Go old school and record them in a journal. This doesn't have to be anything elaborate or fancy. Inexpensive coil-bound Hilroy notebooks work beautifully. This journal is for your eyes only. It's private and personal. What you write here is up to you. Things you're grateful for, things that you're worried about, things that frighten the shit out you, things that keep you awake, things you want to manifest, things that make you happy, things you want to change, things you want to do, things you dream about, all the things big and small. Get it all down Girl Warrior. Devote about a page every day to this practice. Date it, close it and tuck it away for 24 hours.

After journaling, move your body. First indoors and then get outside if you can. This is important. Even if you plan to go to the gym or a yoga class or run at the end of the day, take time to do some gentle harmonious exercise as part of your early morning routine. You may not be able to leave your home if you have kid responsibilities but you can do 30 minutes of soft bending, stretching and strengthening to honor your body. If you can get outside after your indoor practice, go for a walk or run in the early morning light. Everything looks and smells and feels so different at that hour. The ordinary becomes extraordinary. If you can't get out, throw open the windows and breathe in the outdoors, the fresh air, listen to the heartbeat of the Earth. It's fucking glorious.

When this gentle activity is done, hydrate some more, enjoy a healthy breakfast and savor this peaceful time of solitude and awakening. After you have gifted yourself this time of self-devotion you are ready to embrace the day joyfully, confidently and optimistically. You'll have more to give in all arenas of your life—family, friends, colleagues and community—more intelligence, more creativity, more ideas, more energy, more kindness, more patience, more love.

This is what happens Girl Warrior when you take the time—every single day—to fill the well.

Stay in Your Own Lane.

Stay in your own lane. Focus on the task at hand. Concentrate fully on what you want to achieve and accomplish right here and now. Make this your priority. Pay attention. Be alert. Remain vigilant.

Don't be sidetracked or derailed by the people, places or things that have nothing to do with this particular project or undertaking. This won't be easy in a world of non-stop distraction. But you're up for the challenge and you don't need easy when you've got drive and determination in your hip pocket.

There will always be someone cutting into your lane, requesting a piece of you. But if you want to fulfill your dreams and reach your goals then you'll need to push aside the extraneous noise, enticing diversions, idle amusements, and yes, even all those guilty pleasures. At least for the time being. Or for however long it takes to arrive at your destination.

Girl, don't worry about what's going on in someone else's lane either. That's none of your business. Quit peeking. Craning your neck. Taking a gander. Glancing over your shoulder. Or worse yet, surreptitiously spying on the performance, power or presentation of others. And most importantly, stop comparing. That's a fool's game. So shut that shit down immediately.

Instead, remind yourself of just how incomparable you are Girl Warrior. And keep your eyes on the road ahead, as you cruise down the highway of infinite possibilities.

Stop Being a Nice Girl.

Girl Warrior, stop being such a nice girl. A good girl. A sweet girl. Flush that sugar and spice and all things nice crap down the proverbial toilet along with all the pink cupcakes, sky-high-heels, rom-coms and pom-poms. Take the cotton candy and honey pie out of your vernacular and shove it in that spectacular place where the sun don't shine.

These may be enjoyable things to eat, watch or wear but they have precious little to do with who you really are. You are way more than this. And being way more than this, being authentic, speaking your truth, working your inside out just may piss some people off. Offend others. Shock and surprise more than a few. Send some running in the opposite direction. Even the ones that supposedly held you in high regard or loved you unconditionally.

Girl Warrior, stop hiding your bad girl. Defiant girl.

Naughty girl. Your gloriously feisty, unruly and rebellious girl. Bring her out of the closet, out of the bathroom, from under the bed, from under the rug, out of the box and most importantly, out of containment. Remove her from wherever it is that you stash your most valuable possessions, best-kept secrets and venerable treasures.

Unleash her. Unearth her. Cut the tether. Set her free. And bring her into the light.

Let her speak her mind. Without reserve, restraint or reticence. Let her express her feelings. Without shame, shyness or suppression. Let her take the biggest badass risks of her life. Fearlessly, ferocious and flagrantly. And when necessary, let her offend, exasperate, irritate, anger, upset, and yes, oh yes, piss people off. Big time.

Girl Warrior, let her substitute affected politeness and people pleasing for radical honesty and extreme integrity.

Engage Your Radical Trifecta.

Engage your Radical R trifecta—Rebel, Revolutionary, and Renegade. Especially during make-or-break times and crucial circumstances, the cliff-edge life-changing moments. This is when you will be well served to marshal your passionate determined ass-kicking spirit. The one that knows intuitively when to break the rules, break through the barriers, break the code, break the habit, and yes, at times, break the hearts.

Throw off the cloak of convention. Step out of the box of ordinary. Walk away from the pedestrian. Steer clear of the middle-of-the-road. Bury the garden-variety. Remove all things plain-vanilla, milk-toast and bland from your physical and spiritual diet.

And most importantly, don't live a life that isn't worth writing home about.

Live a stranger than fiction life Girl Warrior. One you have exclusively authored. A life that no one else but you could possibly conceive much less, write. Live a life that you are so jazzed about, that is so juicy and spicy and ridiculously overflowing with everything good and bad, ugly and pretty, heartbreaking and joyous, messy and meticulous, bitter and sweet, wonderful and scary, unpredictable and unknown, exhausting and exhilarating, breathtaking and beyond.

Living a rich ample life like this necessitates that you go out on a limb; you make big disruptive waves; and do things differently. You don't go with the flow. Or do the logical, the predictable, the rational or sensible.

And above all else girl, you walk the high wire without a safety net. And learn to love it.

Don't Edit.

Resist the urge to constantly edit yourself. Change, if necessary. Improve, yes. Grow, most certainly. Challenge your current state of reality, absolutely. Evolve, positively. Do all these things. Engage fully and passionately in the process of becoming.

But also remember the beautiful being you are. Right here and right now.

While you're on the progress path, realize with every precious scrap of your consciousness that there are wonderful dear things about you that are quintessentially perfect. These are the idiosyncratic things, the singular, sometimes quirky, rare and unusual characteristics that you, and only you, possess. No one else can claim ownership of these truly marvelous qualities. Remember that.

Herein lies your X-Factor. The 'je ne sais quoi' of you.

The distinctive trademark that no one else can copy, duplicate, replicate, plagiarize, pirate, poach or clone. Your bona fide stamp, your permanent tattoo, your indelible birthmark. Don't hold something like this back. Flaunt it.

So wear your bedazzling Lone Ranger brooch Girl Warrior, and let it shine. Loud and proud. No editing. No paring back. No curtailing. No reining in or diminishing. No not ever.

Don't Walk Away.

Don't walk away or turn your head when you see someone you find displeasing, disdainful or off-putting. Or worse. Repugnant. Repulsive. Revolting. The homeless beggar, the panhandler, the vagrant or vagabond. And especially, the shabby-dirty-raggedy-ass-down-and-out-nasty derelict, bum or bag lady.

Don't inflict an egregious unkindness by pretending you didn't see or that they weren't there. Don't turn this Human Being into one of the Invisible Souls. By turning away you are actually saying, 'you don't matter. I am better than you.'

Instead, lean into compassion, empathy, and understanding. And know this: but for the grace of God goes all of us, including you Girl Warrior. You are not above the fray and beyond reproach.

Instead, love the unlovable. Love those who the world has discarded. Love those who have been cast aside, tossed out, left abandoned. Or worst of all, the ones we have given up on: the hopeless cases and the unfixable.

Instead, open your loving divine heart and express your beautiful humanity. Allow your natural tenderness to well up and occupy your spirit until it is filled to the brim and overflowing. Then take all of this abundant goodness and give this very personal gift to the one standing on the street corner, hat in hand. Or the one slumped against a storefront holding a cardboard sign with a scribbled message that reads simply, but oh so elegantly, 'please help.'

Say yes, yes, yes Girl Warrior. Say yes, I will help.

Never Give Up.

Never give up Girl Warrior. No matter what. Go get all the wonderful and truly wicked things you want out of this life. Chase unapologetically after your dreams. Pursue them persistently. Passionately. Purposefully.

Follow your bliss. Wherever it takes you. This is your quest. All yours Girl Warrior. Imagine that, Beautiful Butterfly.

There will be obstacles in your path. Guaranteed. Roadblocks. Landslides. Washouts. Detours, diversions and distractions. All kinds of barriers, hurdles and little sneaky snags. It's okay if you trip and fall when you hit one of these. Your job is to get back in the saddle, on the bike, behind the wheel, on your feet. Don't hesitate when this happens. Steady yourself. Stay on course. Reset your sights if need be. Do whatever it takes. The idea is to keep heading in the direction of your brass ring.

Keep your wits about you. Not everyone will get what you're doing. Along the way you'll encounter dream crushers and naysayers. These are easy to spot because they are the ones who are quick to squash, smash and suppress the desires of your brave lion-heart. Shut their voices down quickly and carry on. The tougher ones are the well-meaning folks, who for whatever reason, don't get behind your calling. Wish these people well, bless them, love them, and move on.

Know that you are tougher than any storm. There isn't anything you can't weather. Go out there and be some-one's pain in the ass. Be the squeaky wheel that insists on being oiled. Be tenacious. Courageous. Audacious. Strong-willed and stubborn as a mule if need be.

But always be patiently persistent. Remember this on the dark days. It will pay off big-time in the end Girl Warrior.

Don't Waste Your Pretty.

Don't waste your pretty on anyone who is unworthy. Consider that thought for a moment. Let it sink in. Allow it to ooze into the deepest place inside your generous heart and beautiful mind. For it is here that you will know the truth.

And the truth is Girl Warrior you are one fabulous chick.

You deserve to be surrounded by sweet heart-stopping goodness. Pure and simple. Drop anything less than that like a bad habit. Kick their sorry ass to the curb. Don't wave or blow a kiss goodbye. Put them in your rear view mirror. Permanently. Save all your heavenly kisses for the good ones. For they are out there just waiting for your warm embrace.

Be radical about this knowledge. Wrap your brilliant

brain around this information. Fill your soul with this awareness. Grasp the importance of this concept. And hold onto this big idea for dear life.

Seek extravagant love. The best love. The kind of love that is true to the marrow. That sees, with breathtaking clarity, your pretty in all its magical complicated layers. The kind of love that holds like crazy-glue. No matter what.

Because girl, your pretty is too precious to be unappreciated.

Work Hard.

Dream big Girl Warrior. In ultra-high-definition. Of epic proportions. Beyond the beyond of the beyond. Without brims, borders or boundaries.

100   The sky isn't even the limit when it comes to your dreams Girl Warrior. That's just for starters. Your little aspiration appetizer. Amuse-bouche. Take these dreams of yours to the moon and back, from here to infinity, and then some. See what happens.

And don't stop at just one. Have so many dreams your heart and mind and spirit cannot contain them. Break all the rules here. There is no magic number. You are not born with a finite quantity. In fact, it's quite the opposite. Dreams are designed to be an embarrassment of riches.

These sweet dreams are the beautiful seeds that grow the beautiful you.

And always remember that you are the star of your dreams. They belong to you. They are the essential element of your blockbuster kick-ass tale. And absolutely crucial to your never-ending life story. These supernatural keys unlock every door of opportunity. Every possibility, promise and potential begins here. And the best thing is, they are yours to shape and mold and refine in any way that pleases you. Plus the bonus bit is, you can change your dreams at any time you choose. That's the beauty of it. Nothing's ever really locked in.

So start dreaming Girl Warrior. And blow the roof off this place.

Watch What You Say.

Watch what you say, especially to yourself Girl Warrior. Pay attention to your inner dialogue. The relentless non-stop conversation you have inside your head. The bitter discourses, fiery discussions and heated debates that turn and churn like a broken record in your mind. All the random thoughts that come and go but have such a powerful impact on the person you are. And more importantly, on the person you will become.

You are what you think, girl. And what you think you are is in essence who you are. Every second, of every minute, of every day, your self-talk shapes your reality. For better or for worse. It's critical that you understand that your exterior world is actually your interior world manifested. Everything around you begins as an inside job. Think about that. Ponder the potency of that idea and just how empowering it truly is.

So first and foremost, don't tell lies to yourself. Like I'm not good enough. Not smart enough. Not talented enough. Not pretty enough. Not enough of anything. Stop the self-condemnation and self-flagellation. Stop all the crazy-making put-downs and criticism. Stop saying all the hurtful things you would never say to anyone else. Stop the little inside bully. Right here and now.

Stop.

And instead, tell yourself the honest truth. The brave and fearless bloodletting truth. You are more than good enough. You are smart. You are beautiful. You are a brilliant. You are talented. You are tough. You are courageous. You are loving. You are kind. You are gentle. You are strong. You are large-hearted. You are a force to be reckoned with. You are spectacular in every way. You are a Pink Stone Diamond. The rarest of rare.

Tell yourself all that Girl Warrior. And only that.

Help One Another.

Help one another Girl Warrior. By doing so you elevate everyone. You all rise to a loftier place. Reach that higher ground of understanding, compassion, empathy and healing. You have this power, not only in your hands, but also in your great big expansive heart. This is one of the most profound secrets to accomplishing great things.

Go out into the world shoulder to shoulder. Hand in hand. Side-by-side. Create a brighter future. Together.

Be there when called upon. Be there when and where you are needed. Be there when it's achingly difficult. Be there in good times and in bad. Be there even when it's inconvenient or uncomfortable. Be the girl you'd want in your corner, to have your back, when life delivers its worst blows or finest triumphs.

Be that girl.

See your face in the face of other girls. Although they may look differently, don't be fooled by exteriors, by facades or appearances, for they are Girl Warriors just like you. They have dreams and plans and visions for their lives. Exquisite minds. Magnificent intelligence. Beautiful brains. You aren't merely sisters with traveling pants. You are sisters with traveling spirits that transcend the limitations of time and place. You are connected and united in more ways than you may realize. And you can make an enduring difference. You possess the power to change things.

105

Know this.

None of this is easy work. No small feat. Not for the faint-hearted. But you are a Girl Warrior. You are cut from a different cloth. You are not only up for the task but you were born for it. It's tailor-made and designed just for you. So go out and celebrate one another. Applaud, cheer, praise, encourage, comfort, inspire, motivate, support, respect, and above all, love one another.

Reach out. Extend your hand. Help each other. Not only to get through this life but to create a life that is mind-blowingly extraordinary. Beyond your widest imaginings.

Go girl. Go now and handcraft a brighter future.

Be Resilient.

Be resilient Girl Warrior. Flexible. Pliable. Adapt-
able. Bend and sway like an elegant willow tree. Full of
grace and economy. Follow the ebb and flow of your
wonderful awe-inspiring life. Embrace the wind that
moves your sturdy spirit. Take courageous steps into the
blinding light and the dark places of your soul. There is
nothing to fear.

You are stronger than you think Girl Warrior.

You are hard-wearing and tough. Like an indestructible
black leather jacket. But you are also supple and nimble.
Like a Ninja cat. Both contain the secret to resiliency at
its finest.

Study intently the skill of quick recovery. Practice dili-
gently irrepressible comebacks. Master the fine art of give
and take. Rise from the ashes like the magnificent Phoenix

you are. Rally and return stronger and more resourceful than you could ever imagine.

But remember girl, it's not an all or nothing life that we live. That's the true wisdom in resilience.

Put on your cape.
And fly.

Have a Grateful Heart.

Have a grateful heart Girl Warrior. Count your blessings. Each and every day. There are so many things to appreciate in your life. Right here and now. Take nothing for granted. Don't squander your godsend.

Concern yourself with all the things you already have. Not with what's missing or what you don't have or wished you had. For if you aren't grateful for what you already possess then getting more of anything else won't change your heart or fill your soul.

Know this Girl Warrior, it is imperative that you are first and foremost grateful for the life you have, the gorgeous gift that it is. Look around at the people who surround you and give thanks for their presence. See the heavenly divineness in all things. Big and small. It's all so precious.

See your cup half full. Always. Express your thanks at

every turn. Seek opportunities to acknowledge the lavishness of your life. Just as it is in this precise moment. Look around at the eternal abundance of the universe. And say thank you. Make this your mantra.

Send out Thank You cards to the world Girl Warrior.

Celebrate.

Celebrate Girl Warrior. Everything. And anything. You can always find a reason. Take a moment every day to honor and take pleasure in something. Even the smallest and simplest. The stuff that's so easy to overlook. The outwardly ordinary. The seemingly run-of-the-mill. Start here and let it grow. Like a heaven-sent happiness seed.

You woke up. You're alive. You've been blessed with another day to give this life your best shot. A clean slate. A fresh beginning. Another day to dream and scheme and breathe utter brilliance into every single thing you do. Take note and rejoice in that astounding thought.

Make every day a special occasion. No matter where you are or who you're with. Enjoy every second. Whoop and holler. Party hardy. Live it up. Have a ball. Kick up your heels. Be silly and make a fabulous fool of yourself. Let things get insanely messy. Eat drink and be merry. Dress up and go out on the town. Or throw a pajama party for all your besties. Celebrate your friendship, your sisterhood, and all those you hold near and dear. Crack open a bottle of wine or a bottle of pop. Dunk Oreos in milk. Make bread and break bread. Have big wonderful meals together. Or snuggle two-by-two. Make hot chocolate with extra marshmallows and read a good book. Celebrate your priceless alone time too.

Celebrate the holidays, special occasions and all the magnificent milestones along the way. Don't let them slip carelessly by unnoticed. For these are the markers of your life. The things you'll look back on that will make you smile and fill your heart with joy and gratitude. These are the essentials of memory making. The lumps in your throat, the flutter in your heart, and the shiny tears in your eyes. These are your finest happy pills.

Girl, cherish the gift of celebration all the days of your life. You will never be too old.

Listen Up.

Listen up Girl Warrior. Listen attentively and actively when someone is speaking to you. Listen empathically. Sympathetically. Conscientiously. Listen with your ears. Listen with your eyes. Listen with your heart. Engage all your senses. And your extra senses also.

Give all your attention to the one doing the talking. Whether they have come to pour their heart out and confide in you. Or pour you a cup of tea and all that is required is some comfortable conversation with a cookie.

Focus on the one across from you. Do not allow yourself to become distracted, diverted or drawn away. Don't let anything trump or eclipse this moment between you. Turn off your cell phone. Close your tablet. Shut down your laptop. Turn off the TV. And tune in.

Then lean in. Look hard into their eyes. Let them

know they matter. What they have to say matters. Their thoughts and feelings and fears and hopes and dreams count for something. This is important stuff, girl. Respect, regard and reverence are composed and crafted here in these everyday exchanges. These ordinary little tête-à-têtes that happen so often we take them for granted. These soulful heart-to-hearts that we assume will always be. But the truth is, they won't. So don't squander even one single solitary conversation by not being fully present.

Girl Warrior let the one across from you know that you have not only shown up, but you are fully engaged. And listening.

Don't Judge.

Girl Warrior resist the urge to judge. Criticize. Condemn. Crucify. Cast aspersions or make snap decisions about the words or deeds of others. Not everything is as it appears on the surface. Nor at first blush. Outward appearances are often deceiving.

We all have a backstory that affects the present-day things that we do or think or say. And some backstories aren't so rosy. Glowing halos do not hover above everyone's head. For some, the crown of light has been dimmed or extinguished completely. And there is no glory. The reasons for this loss of luminosity matters not.

What matters girl, is that you take a step back. And ditch any self-righteous attitude. Holier-than-thou posturing. False feelings of moral superiority. Shake loose the sanctimonious, smug and self-satisfied belief that you are better than the girl next to you, the one down the road, or across the world. Instead take a walk in another's earth-worn shoes. You may find their pain unbearable. Enduring one single step impossible, much less going a mile.

For this, and only this, will allow you the grace to see things from a different perspective. To hear the true meaning in the silence between the words. To fully understand that there is usually more to the story.

And always remember this, kind and loving Girl Warrior, judgment is a door that swings both ways.

Press Pause.

Press pause Girl Warrior. Give yourself a time out. Take a break. A breather. Remove yourself from the busyness of life. Especially when you feel you have no time to do so. For that is when you need it the most.

Step away from the chaos that surrounds you. Separate yourself from all the noise and nonsense. Beat a hasty retreat from the racket and wild rumpus. Clear the incessant commotion inside your head that's tearing your fragile spirit to shreds. And wreaking havoc with your overloaded senses.

Stop the madness Girl Warrior. Check out of Hotel Crazy. Find your place of refuge. We all have a sacred space, a thinking spot, and a place where peace is waiting. Go there. If you don't have one, find one or create one. It's that important. And once there, take the time you need to revive, rejuvenate and refresh. Breathe new life into your weary bones.

Resist the urge to overthink or complicate things. Finding a place to rest and recover can be as easy as drawing a hot bath filled with your favorite fragrance, locking the door to the outside world, lighting a few candles, pouring a beverage that nurtures your spirit, and closing your eyes as you sink into the sweet soothing serenity of silence.

Then just let it all go girl. Let it go.

Foster Wisdom.

Foster Wisdom Girl Warrior. Seek enlightenment, illumination and insight at every turn. Grow your intuition and awareness of the world around you and the one within. Fine-tune your instincts and your vital sixth sense. Follow your hunches and listen closely to your gut feelings. For these are the essential bits in the Sage's toolkit.

First you will need to take a journey inward. You will also need to open your mind to all the possibilities that abide there. You will be opening the door to the unknown, the unexplored, the unfamiliar, and above all else, the uncertain. You will be knocking on the door of mystery and magic and all things mystical. The prospect of this may frighten you. Don't let it. Open the door and walk unflinchingly through. This is a big step and a brave move on your part. But it is a prerequisite on the path to true understanding.

It is here that you will begin to know the difference between the accumulation of information and knowledge and that of wisdom, knowing and genuine insight. It is in this pilgrimage to the deepest aspect of your soul that you will discover the Universal Truths, your highest self, your eternal self and your infinite connection to the Divine. It is from this vantage point that you will do your best work.

It is both exalting and humbling. And when you get there, girl you will know.

Take Good Care of Your Skin.

Take good care of your skin Girl Warrior. You are never too young to begin a daily routine. This is the outer layer of your Earth Suit and it needs loving-kindness every bit as much as your heart and mind and spirit, your muscles and bones, your blood and sinew. It's what you present to the world initially and it always makes a first impression whether you like it or not. But the beautiful thing is you have the power to make this perception good if you choose to.

This isn't about looks or appearances—although if you do look after your epidermis you will definitely reap the benefits—it's about health and wellbeing. It has absolutely nothing to do with vanity. Your skin is the largest organ and it has the very big job of protecting your inner being. Every second that you walk this good earth it is doing exactly what it needs to do to preserve, maintain and sustain you Girl Warrior. But it does need you to do your part.

It's pretty simple really. You didn't get this far without knowing the drill. The secret to achieving a Cleopatra-like complexion isn't that complicated. There's no mystery here. It's all about habits. Good ones. Daily ones. Circadian ones. It's about mindfulness and awareness, practice and routine.

And it's about knowing and abiding by these basic rules.

Moisturize. Moisturize. Moisturize. Start your day with a clean palette and smear on your favorite face cream and body lotion. Don't step out the door without protection. Take off all your makeup at the end of the day. No matter what. No exceptions to this rule. Then moisturize. Moisturize. Moisturize. And remember, while you're in the Land of Nod your skin is exercising its super healing powers. So remove the residue and remnants of the day and get your beauty sleep.

Be good to your skin, girl. It needs to last a lifetime.

Respect Yourself.

Respect yourself Girl Warrior. Yes you. Hold yourself in high regard. The highest, in fact. For you are a prized and precious and perfect person. Exactly as you are now. Exactly as you always have been. And exactly as you always will be.

This does not mean you won't change and grow. Refine, reshape and rework your life. You'll expand, emend and evolve as you go. There will be times when you press repeat, rewind or even pause. And that's okay. You'll learn new things. Astonishing things that will blow your mind. You are free to try on different roles and responsibilities along the highway or dirt road of your one-of-a-kind odyssey. Abandon what doesn't feel right in your skin. Keep all that speaks to your truth and honors the brilliant Girl Warrior that you are. For this is the essence of self-respect.

Respecting yourself is part and parcel of loving yourself. It all starts here. You unwrap them together. They are hand in glove and should not be separated. They will act as your guide, your touchstone and spiritual litmus test for everything you think, say and do. But they do ask that you think well of yourself at all times. That you hold yourself in such high regard and esteem that you wouldn't think of causing harm to yourself. Not physically. Not emotionally. Not intellectually. Not spiritually. Not ever.

There are no exceptions, girl. Your standard is set high. It is golden. And so are you.

Don't Take Offense.

Don't take offense Girl Warrior. This may be one of your greatest challenges. One you'll not only need to work on every day but possibly every minute of every day. For being offended, insulted or indignant by another's words or deeds happens so easily. Sticks and stones may break the bones. But words can hurt. Deeply. Profoundly. Irreparably.

Thoughtless, unkind or flippant words are often the most harmful to our psyche, to our spirit, to our soul; but only if we allow or give them permission to do so. Therein lies our power. Therein lies our potency. Therein lies our potential. We are at the controls here. This is our command central. How we feel. How we think. How we react. And most importantly, how we act after receiving such a blow is everything. This is the "big tell." More is revealed about our character than about that of the transgressor.

Our egos are bruised. Our hearts are broken. Our feelings are hurt. Our spirits deflated.

But they needn't be. Know this Girl Warrior, you have the power to A) neutralize your emotions and B) control your response. Both are critical and integral here. You don't have to be upset, insulted, angry or wounded. You are not a victim. In fact you are just the opposite. What others say to you, or about you, is actually none of your business. Others will say or do what they will, often without even realizing the impact or the consequences. And so will you. So will you. That's the hard pill to swallow. We are all guilty.

But you can fix this, girl. It is your job, your mission, to get at the truth and own it. And then forgive everyone, including yourself, so healing can begin. For that is how you get over being offended.

Surrender All.

Surrender all Girl Warrior. Let go of all the junk that litters your beautiful life. This includes everything. Externally and internally. Release all the things that break your heart, your mind and ultimately, your precious soul.

Change what you can. Clean house when you can. Chuck out all the clutter wherever you can. Clear away as much of the chaos and confusion that is causing you stress and suffering, anguish and agony, distress and disease. Do all that is necessary to rid yourself of negativity. Say farewell to the three isms—cynicism, criticism and pessimism—in yourself, in others, in situations, and in circumstances.

Put on your fiercest boots and kick away. Stomp hard and stomp fast. Do what you have to, to set yourself free from these physical, emotional and spiritual crushers.

But be warned girl, this may also mean you have to say goodbye to some people, places, things and thinking. Yes, thinking. And this may not be easy. Loosening the grip, uncurling the fist, severing the tie is grueling work. But it is also gratifying.

Girl Warrior, now stand up and take a long hard look at your world, the one you have created. Is it as good as you can make it, at least for today? Have you done all you can? Given it your best shot? Tried the hardest you possibly could? If the answer is yes, then drop to your knees. Kiss the ground. Exhale fully and let it all go.

Then slip into sweet sweet surrender.

Don't be a Shrinking Violet.

Don't be a shrinking violet Girl Warrior. Ever. No, not ever. Not for any reason. Not for any person. Not in any situation. Under no circumstances or conditions.

130   Do not make yourself small. Do not diminish, draw back or decrease in any way your presence on this planet. For it belongs to you as much as it does any other. You have a place here. A position to defend. A stand to take. A clear and resounding voice. Let it be heard. For it is utterly magnificent.

Don't back away from the good fight. Don't abandon your convictions. Or betray your beliefs, ideologies or principles. Don't let fear or any other false fabrication of your imagination prevent you from being the big girl that you are. Don't let anyone tell you that you are too big for your britches. That's impossible. Stay vigilant and ignore ludicrous comments designed to keep you in your place. Or worse yet, keep you down.

You have big things to do, girl. Brilliant things. Bright things beyond your wildest dreams. But doing these things will require you to step out boldly and bravely into every arena as the formidable force that you are.

So put on your big gutsy attitude, girl and show the world what it looks like to be too damn big for your britches.

Ask and You Shall Receive.

Ask and you shall receive Girl Warrior. On the surface this is such a simple concept. Easy peasy pudding and pie. You know this. But do you really? Do you get it right down deep in your gut and marrow? The places where your truth lives, where the things that matter most take flight, where your greatness is born.

Understanding the brilliance and pixie dust of asking is a big game changer.

Take a moment, girl and imagine the life you want to manifest. Picture all the things you want to have or do or see—all the magnificent people you want to draw into your world, all the places your soul beckons, and all the personal and professional boundaries you want to bust through. Think about all those fantastical things you wish and hope for and go to sleep dreaming about.

Is the astonishing life you want achievable on your own? Probably not. We're all on the Good Ship Lollipop together and we need each other. Big time. The help you seek may only be one question away.

What's stopping you? Is it fear?

Are you fearful of your requests? Fearful of your desires, your needs and your intense yearnings. Fearful of your hunger and all the things in life that you crave, covet, lust and thirst for. Are you fearful that your requests will fall on mocking ears, scornful ears, or worse yet, deaf ears? That your impassioned appeals will go unanswered. Do you fear that your gorgeous tender heart will break from the silence, rage and fury that beat within?

Do you ask who is listening? Who will answer? You will never know, girl unless you have the courage to ask. And if you don't ask, you won't ever get.

You Have the Right to Say Yes and to Say No.

You have the right to say yes and to say no Girl Warrior. You always have a choice. Always. It's critical that you understand the importance of this. Especially at those times when you hit the fork in the road and a decision must be made. If not your life, then your wellbeing could depend on it.

It's your life, your body, and your mind. It is all sacredly yours to decide how what where when and why you will use it as a means of expression. Only you get to decide what happens to you. This point is a powerful pill. Take it in massive doses.

Do not let anyone tell you differently. Do not grant permission to another living soul. Do not surrender your esteemed self. Do not allow another to pressure, persuade or push you into anything you do not want to do. Do not let anyone sweet-talk you into being untrue to the self-respecting warrior that you are. Do not enable arm-twisting of any kind.

No matter what.

Do exercise your right to self-determination. Do grow all your spiritual muscles around this notion. Do expand your understanding of the things that matter most to you. Do figure out who belongs on your odyssey and who does not. Do take control of your life. Do manifest your own destiny.

Girl, whether it's yes or no, the choice belongs to you. Only you.

It's Okay to Fail.

It's okay to fail Girl Warrior. In fact, it's okay to fail repeatedly. Over and over and over. It's not the end of the world. Not a catastrophe. Nor a disaster. Never just plain bad luck. It can be quite the opposite, depending on your perspective.

Tweak the lens of your defeatist frame of mind and you will have the power to see things in a different light. Not the end, but the beginning. A mere setback, not the end of the road. Do this and you will begin to see the doors and windows of opportunity fling open wide. Just for you.

The catastrophe becomes your good fortune. A disaster leads to your unparalleled success. Bad luck turns into your most profound blessing. You get to experience the awesome wonder of Divine Grace. You get to hear the Heavenly Whisperer's promise that failing does not make you a failure. It makes you beautifully human. It is simply grooming you to fulfill your Girl Warrior destiny.

Try. Try. And try again. With each attempt you are one step closer to achieving all of your hopes and dreams and wishes and everything your passionate heart desires. All that you crave and hunger and yearn for draws closer and closer. Everything is within reach and ultimately achievable if you are determined, tenacious, resolute, persevering, patient, unwavering and unshakable. Be like the dog with a bone.

And know this girl, that when you fail you are never alone. A loving, faithful and supportive tribe, who are your collective safety net, surrounds you. And you will always, always, always have a soft and safe place to land.

Know When to Take Off the Kid Gloves.

Know when to take off the kid gloves Girl Warrior. This comes with a warning, as it isn't as easy as it sounds. Especially when it comes to our beloved tribe. And ourselves.

138   Our natural instinct is to be kind, loving, supportive and magnanimous of spirit. Our innate tendency is towards being nice, polite, agreeable and well behaved. We want to be liked. We don't want to offend. Hurt someone's feelings. Make another angry. Or worse yet, abandon us.

But at what cost Girl Warrior?

What do we lose by handling each other like Delicate Flowers? Does walking on eggshells really resolve issues? Is our skin really that thin? Are we so fragile that hearing the truth, and nothing but the truth, will break us? Is the fear that our authentic and genuine-selves is so unlovable that we'll scare everyone away even those nearest and dearest?

No. None of this is true. We are not Delicate Flowers. We are not fragile, frail or feeble. Fear not. Have faith in yourself to speak from the wise and higher place within. And trust that the one hearing your words is there with you. Know that you are both strong enough to give and take a little tough talk.

Girl, sometimes the most sensitive, kind and caring messages are the ones delivered when the kid gloves are off.

This Too Shall Pass.

This too shall pass Girl Warrior. Impossible to believe when you're in the heat of the battle or in the eye of the storm. In the hour of the wolf when only the devil knows your name. When you cry out into the darkness begging for mercy. You're down on your knees praying for your misery to end. Your heart is breaking and your body is aching. You hurt everywhere.

You are in agony. You feel alone. Lost. Abandoned. Hopeless.

The emotional or physical pain is so unbearable you wonder if you will ever feel normal again. You can't see two inches in front of you, much less the light at the end of the tunnel. You are unable to feel the warmth of a sunny day. You wonder, will you ever laugh again? Will your spirit be carefree once more? Will your burden be lifted?

Yes, Girl Warrior. Yes.

Relief from your suffering will come. Be assured. But it will take time, and patience, tenderness, gentleness, kindness. You will find these in the embrace of your Dear Ones, who will love you unconditionally in your vulnerability and brokenness. Bit-by-bit. Day-by-day. One foot in front of the other, you will get there. You will be whole.

Life will never be what it was girl. It will be better. Because you not only survived, you thrived.

Spend Time with a Mentor.

Spend time with a mentor Girl Warrior. If you don't have one, find one. Chances are, this person is already in your life. Chances are, you've already engaged in a mentor-mentee relationship. Chances are, you may not recognize that you are connected in this way. Chances are, you are close to this person.

Take a look around you and ask yourself these questions.

Who is the person you admire most? Who is the person who teaches you things in a manner that feels natural rather than professorial, purposive or patronizing? Who is the person who leaves you feeling uplifted after spending time with them? Who is the person who challenges you to think beyond what you know now? Who is the person who encourages you to grow fully in every capacity—physically, spiritually, intellectually? Who is the person who has your best interests at heart? Who is the person who tells you the truth in a way that doesn't hurt or harm? Who is the person you want to be like when you grow up?

Girl Warrior, take a moment to write down the name of the person next to each of these questions. Chances are, this is your mentor. If you're lucky, more than one name will crop up. But even if it is only one person, consider yourself blessed.

Now, go to that person and tell them how grateful you are to have them in your life. If you aren't physically close to them then pick up the phone, text them, email them, send them a letter or a "thank-you" card. Do not put this off. It is imperative that you acknowledge whom your mentors are and that they know how much you value their presence in your life. Let them know now that the world is a better place because they are here. This is the very personal gift that you give back to them.

Once you have done this girl, take a second look around and ask yourself this. Who can I mentor?

Don't Settle.

Don't settle Girl Warrior. Go along with, resign or reconcile yourself, stomach, swallow or submit to anything that doesn't ring true to the bright and shiny person you are.

Don't live a default life. A 'learn to live with' life. An involuntary life. Or worse yet, one that belongs to someone else. And you're just going along for the ride. Sitting complacently, but maybe not so comfortably, in the back seat or sidecar. You belong behind the wheel of your own life, the one of your own making. Steer your spaceship courageously in the direction of your dreams. Not someone else's. That's your mission, your primary assignment here.

You only get to do this present-life thing one time, and one time only, girl. And it is oh so very brief. So fleeting. A flutter of the butterfly's wing. Yes, some things are eternal. Our souls. The tender memories of us. But this here-and-now Earth Walk, and all the glorious people, places and things that are gifted to us are here for such a woefully brief time. So don't squander any of it by settling.

Don't settle in. Don't settle down. Don't settle for. Anything. And that goes for the people in your life, the work you do, the place where you live, the man or woman you're involved with, and most importantly, the desires of your heart.

Girl, don't be afraid that if you choose not to settle you'll be all alone. You won't. Quite the opposite is true. You'll be surrounded by your loving and brave Tribe of kindred spirits who also refused to settle for anything less than an authentic life.

Don't waste your pretty on anyone who is unworthy.

Judgment is a door that swings both ways.

Get Enough Sleep.

Get enough sleep Girl Warrior. Make this a top priority every night. And you will have better days. Guaranteed.

You live a busy 24-7 life. Always on the go. You're stretched to the max most days. Demands are flying at you from every direction. You put others' needs before your own. You're on stress and strain overload. Worry, anxiety and pressure greet you at every turn. Everyone wants a piece of you.

And quite simply, you are running on empty.

When you get to this exhausting place girl, it's time to re-fuel. Truth is, this isn't really an option. Not when your health and wellbeing are at stake. It's time to shut it all down and take good care of yourself. And the best place to do this is in the bedroom.

This is your sanctuary, your peaceful retreat, and most importantly, your recovery refuge. Think calm, serene, tranquil and relaxing. So feather your nest in a way that fosters these feelings. Make it comfortable and cozy, safe and snug. Free of all distractions and disturbances. Make this a place for you to rest your weary bones and leave all the cares of the day behind.

Hang a Do Not Disturb sign on the door of your mind.

Begin a 'get ready for bed' ritual. Make this a habit you can't live without. This is personal so it won't look the same for all Girl Warriors. This matters not. What does matter is that you make it a nightly routine that helps you prepare for sleep. Start by slowing things down. Dim the lights, do some gentle yoga stretches, drink herbal tea, take a warm bath, listen to relaxing music, read a book, meditate, say your prayers and give thanks for all your many blessings and the abundance in your life.

Slip into your divinely inviting bed and allow the healing of your body, mind and spirit to begin. Sweet sweet dreams girl.

Define Your Own Success.

Determine your own definition of what being successful means Girl Warrior. Like many of the big things you'll do, this is an inside job. Start there. Take a long hard close look inwards at the person you are today. The one you were yesterday, last week, last month, last year, or as many years back as your memory will take you.

Then ask yourself this question. Who is this person?

Chances are, this person is somewhere on the growth chart between 'not quite there yet' and 'done like dinner.' Regardless of where you stand on the Spectrum of Light (SOL) you are incomparably perfect. Not flawless. Not without blemishes or warts. Not pristine. But perfect, not in spite of these things but because of them.

With this perspective in mind, and under your own personal magnifying glass, go in closer to see all the people, places and things that truly matter to you. What inspires your soul? Fills your mind with wonder and curiosity? Makes your heart flutter with happiness. Brings tears of joy to your eyes? Scares the shit right out of you? What drives and propels you forward? What makes you want to get up in the morning? What would you rather be doing more than anything else? What does an ideal day look like? Who do you like to be with? Who's in your tribe and who's missing that you wish was there? How do you find bliss? Where do you want to go? When do you start living your life? Why does it matter? And, the really great big huge colossal critical question, why are you here?

Once you have probed deeply and truthfully into the answers to these soul-searching questions, you can start to formulate a picture of what success means to you. Notice that these are questions you ask of yourself. This is a very personal quest and is nobody else's business. Not your parents, friends, teachers, therapists, colleagues, pop icons, social media stars, fashion freaks, political leaders or anyone else that you may be under the influence. Not their life. Not their definition. Not this time.

Know this, being successful lies in your answers to these

vital life-affirming questions. Only these. It's not about wealth or power or influence or status or jobs or fame or fortune or getting ahead or climbing some corporate ladder. It's about loving, honoring and respecting the person looking back at you in the mirror every day. It's about knowing that your presence on Planet Earth matters.

Most importantly girl, it's about knowing that your life is a success because you live it fully and completely, with the utmost integrity and authenticity. And always, always, always according to your own definition. On your terms.

Feel the Pain.

Pain is inevitable Girl Warrior. So feel it. Fully. Thoroughly. Exhaustively. Allow yourself to experience every little detail of the hurt you are experiencing. Physically, mentally and spiritually. Wring your emotions dry.

Purge. Cleanse. Release. Repeat.

There is no escaping pain. You can run but you cannot hide. It affects us all sooner or later. Like death, it happens to everyone and everything. Guaranteed. But unlike death, it doesn't just happen once. And then boom. Lights out. Pain recurs. Also guaranteed.

But what isn't guaranteed is your perspective.

The way you think, feel, react, respond and behave when you're suffering and in your darkest hour. You may not be able to control when something hurtful is going to come your way or cross your path. But you can control what you do when it does.

This isn't easy. Your first impulse may be avoidance. Or denial. Or retreat. You may want to run like hell away from the source of your torment, if you can. Or pull the covers over your head. Bury it in the sand. Lock yourself away. Hold a pity party. Lash out. Make accusations. Lay blame. Threaten to harm yourself. Crush your psyche. Curse at your body or mind. Condemn their betrayal. Give up.

Do these things if you must. And there will be times when you need to do all or some of these things. Recovery, getting rid of the bad shit that happens, is a process. And it takes time to heal wounds. Whether it's a broken arm or a broken heart. A sore knee or a sore spirit. An injured back or an injured mind.

But know girl that eventually you have to face it all. Have a showdown with the pain. Feel it all. Surrender to it all. Accept that it is happening. Because the pain won't leave you until you deal with it. One way or the other. Head-on works. So does a slow and gentle approach. Trust yourself. You actually already know what to do. The wisdom to guide you through this already abides within. Listen to your small quiet voice of truth. Know that all pain is temporary.

Girl, let this pain be one of your quintessential teachers. Learn. Grow. Forgive. Accept. Emerge. Move on.

Say You're Sorry.

Say you're sorry Girl Warrior. When called for. When justified. And most importantly, when the shoe fits. Step up and do the right thing. Without hesitation. Waffling. Or second thoughts. Do not employ any delaying tactics. Avoidance strategies. Stalling for time. And excuse making. Just don't. It only makes things worse. Compounds the hurt. Piles on insult to the original injury.

If you've said something, done something, or caused harm in any way, there is only one course of action. It comes directly out of your mouth and straight from your heart. Three simple little words with profound power. And mighty impact.

Three simple little words that have the capacity to change perspective, rebuild and repair relationships, transform self-esteem, restore good feelings, strengthen bonds, deepen love connections and ultimately provide the greatest gift of all. Heal the heart. The beautiful, breakable, fragile heart that beats within us all.

Three simple little words that should roll easily off the tongue. But so often don't. They get stuck in your throat or on the tip of your tongue. And seem impossible to spit out. No matter how hard you try. Regardless of whether or not you want to say them or know you should. That's not the point. At the end of the day you have to get over yourself, and whatever it is that's holding you back from putting on your big girl pants, and doing the right thing. Saying the three little words that will set you free, girl.

I am sorry.

Set Your
Intentions.

Girl Warrior set your intentions. Start today. Right this minute, here and now. Don't squander or waste another day living a life that isn't your utmost best or reflective of your highest self.

Reach out to the Universe and express in detail exactly and precisely what it is you'd like to see manifest in your world—mentally, physically and spiritually. Body. Mind. Soul. Consider all facets including relationships, family, career, health and wellbeing. It's goal setting on steroids.

This is the first step in creating a happy and fulfilled life or taking it to the next level. This is where you begin. Always. And it's oh so empowering.

There are no right or wrong ways to set your intentions. You can do this through daily meditation, writing in a journal or simple wire-bound notebook, filling a mason jar with aspirational sticky notes, writing your desires in the sand while at the beach, embroidering or cross-stitching inspirational messages on a pillow, painting your plan on a canvas or mural, writing affirmations with lipstick on the mirror you face every morning, constructing a collage or vision board, talking through your objectives with someone your trust.

The ways to do this are endless, personal and as unique as the Girl Warrior expressing them. The idea is to keep things simple and clear and in a language that speaks to you. Language is key here. Everything that comes out of your mouth or that is expressed in some way shape or form is a message and instruction to the Universe.

The cautionary tale here is to speak only what you want to see happen.

Your thoughts and words are filled with extraordinary energy, which becomes everything you see and feel and hear and touch around you. They have the power to transform and bring into being exactly what you tell them to. Good, bad, happy or sad. It's equal parts self-fulfilling prophecy and laws of physics. Science colliding head-on with spirituality and faith.

So girl, communicate all your magnificent intentions and experience firsthand how you transform energy into matter that matters. Believe and you will see.

Piss or Get Off the Pot.

Make this the year you piss or get off the pot Girl Warrior. This is your great big powerful year where you kick all the excuses, delaying tactics, postponing, stalling and deferring to last year's dragging-your-feet to the curb. No more of that. It's done.

The clock is ticking and the truth is there is no more time to waste. Time waits for no man. Or Girl Warrior. So get on with it.

This is the perfect time to pull all your dreams, plans, schemes, resolutions and to-do lists out of the vault and unleash them. This is the perfect time to show the world just exactly what it is you can do. This is the perfect time to rally your troops and all your resources and get some shit done. This is the perfect time for action not reaction. This is the perfect time to become a force to be reckoned with. This is the perfect time to light that fire in your belly. This is the perfect time to take your life to the next level and beyond. This is the perfect time to have the best year of your magnificent life.

What's stopping you, girl?

Take a moment to think about what exactly it is that's holding you back, keeping you from doing all the things you want to do and accomplish. There's probably a lot of negative self-talk and emotional baggage fogging up your beautiful brain and clogging your thinking. It's creative constipation caused by the likes of fear of failure, fear of success, fear of disappointing others, fear of making waves, fear of losing friends or family, fear of being considered a bad girl, fear of being abandoned and left alone, fear of being thought of as crazy. So what.

Say so what to all of those fears.

Odds are, none of it's going to happen anyway. And if it does, you'll deal with it. Head-on and brave-on like you always do. Don't be afraid to be a little bit crazy either. It's the juicy sweet stuff of imagination and innovation. Harness it and make it work on your behalf. Make it crazy vision. Crazy inspiration. Crazy motivation. Crazy inventiveness. Crazy originality. Crazy artistry.

Crazy genius. Crazy love.

So girl, the big question you have to ask yourself, with ruthless honesty, is if not now, when?

Set Your Heart.

Set your heart Girl Warrior. Program it with all your dreams and wishes and desires and wants. Apply it with everything that suits your fancy, along with all the things you plan to achieve during your exquisite, yet ever so brief, time on earth. For this is the sacred and private place for all your yearnings and longings. All your insatiable life-cravings and soul-searching can rest easy here until you are ready to unwrap them. One-by-one.

Try one on. Take it for a test drive. See how it fits and feels. Wear it out. Tuck it in. Wring it dry. Extract every shred of life it holds. Repeat. This could take ten minutes or ten years. Time isn't of the essence here. What matters is that you thoroughly satisfy your hunger, your thirst and your ache for all the things that bring heart and meaning to your life. One-by-one.

Stay meticulously focused on one heart-set at a time.

Make it the sole object of your desire. Love it for all its worth. Nurture it faithfully and give it your unwavering and undivided attention. Keep it crystal clear in your mind's eye. Dust off any and all diversions that keep you from it. And know this. The divided heart is a fractured heart and a fractured heart is fragile or worse yet, broken. That's the last thing you want.

So girl, dig deep and ask yourself, "what is my heart set on today?"

You Gotta Have Faith.

There will be times when you've got to work with the faith others have in you Girl Warrior. Why? Because we don't always see what others see. We don't always have an accurate picture of who we are and what we're capable of. And that false image, that distorted point of view, that illusion cripples us and we become inert. We freeze. Panic. Anxiety courses through our veins. Self-doubt leaks from every pore. Our first thought is that we won't be able to fulfill the request, rise to the occasion and get the job done.

Before we even contemplate, much less try, we entertain fantasies of failure.

But this, Girl Warrior is here to tell you that there are people in your circle of humans, in your tribe, who have a much clearer picture of your strengths and abilities. They include your boss, manager, supervisor, colleague, board director, coach, spiritual leader, spouse, parent, family, friend, neighbor and guru. You know who they are. These are the ones who see the spark of genius. The gifts. Your breathtaking brilliance. They've seen what's inside you. They've seen your mettle. And yes, this may be a test. But it's one you won't fail. Have faith.

Work with that. The next time you're asked to do something—at work, at home, at the place you volunteer or hang out or wherever—that you think is out of your wheelhouse, way beyond anything you're capable of doing or have the specific expertise. Call bullshit on that thought. Suck up the sweat. Take a deep breath and put one foot in front of the other. Act on their faith until your own kicks in. It will.

Here's the final thought girl, you wouldn't have been asked to do "this thing" if you weren't capable of doing it. So, if in that moment you're lacking faith in yourself, say yes and start with the faith that person has in you, because they are right. You can do this.

Plant a Seed.

Dear Girl Warriors,

For the past few weeks I have been trying to think of something to say to you. Something good. Something inspiring. Something helpful. Something.

Then I realized, I got nothing. Nothing.

Until this morning when I woke up. Thank God for that. At the risk of sounding all Pollyanna (if you don't know the reference, look it up), the sun was shining. Shining. In all its glory. Just for me. And you. And you. Yes, you. All of you.

And when you think of it, that's a pretty amazing thing. Profound in magnitude. Because the sun is pretty fucking big. And it makes things grow.

Despite all the scary, tragic things going on in the world, the sun came up this morning. And it shone its light in all the deep dark places my puny mind had succumbed to these past two weeks. It opened my mind to all the possibilities that lie ahead, especially for you, because you are beautiful in every way. Every way possible. It's a simple thought, so take it in. Breathe it in. And spread it around. Let it grow.

You are beautiful in every way. And beautiful Girl Warriors do beautiful things. Things that have a lasting and permanent impact on our families, friends, neighbors, colleagues, community, country and our hurting world. You are that powerful. You are a force to be reckoned with. So don't cower in the face of this particular challenge or any other one coming your way. Because bad shit will always be raining down. Whether it's on you, or someone you don't even know, who lives worlds away. Shit happens.

But after the rain, the sun does come out. It's part of the grand design. A natural wonder. Happens every day. Even when you can't see it. It's there. A daily gift. An optimistic reminder.

That there is hope. Let it grow.

So there it is. My real message to you on this fine sunny morning. Go out and plant a seed Girl Warrior. Literally. Metaphorically. Spiritually. Plant a seed of your choice in the garden of your making. Plant a sunflower seed in your windowsill or garden path. Plant an imagination seed in the creative corner of your wondrous mind. Plant a sacred and everlasting seed of hope in your heart, mind and spirit.

Let all these seeds take hold today Girl Warrior. And watch them grow in the sunshine. And always remember, where there is hope, there is life.

That's it. That's all I got.

Boo

Show the world what it looks like to be too damn big for your britches.

The Remarkable Ones.

Be one of the Remarkable Ones
Take your place among
The Extraordinary
The Exceptional
The mind-blowing Phenoms
The beautiful Freaks
And breathtaking Weirdoes.

Stand shoulder-to-shoulder
With the unflinching Renegades
The fearless Rebels
The Risk-takers
The Soul-shakers
The untamed She-Wolves
And lionhearted Sisters.
Hang out with the Influencers
Who rouse and motivate
The uplifting Inspirers

The gifted Brighteners
The morale Boosters
The clever Quick-witted
And wise Enlightened.

Storm fearlessly into the good night
With your Tribe of Ferocious Sisters
Bare your teeth and growl
Get gritty and wrench your gut
Speak your truth with a deafening roar
Refuse to let your voice be silenced
Because Girl Warrior,
You are one of the Remarkable Ones.

Postscript

Letter to my Girl Warrior Daughters.

Dear A and M,

This is a very personal message from my heart to yours.

This time of year always brings me to a place of reflec-
tion, contemplation and introspection. Maybe it has
something to do with the hint of yellow in the Mani-
toba Maple Tree that shades the window of my creating
space. You know her well.

It's been almost twenty years since I carried her in my
purse across the country from Northwestern Ontario to
Vancouver Island. I felt like a smuggler of precious gems
or illicit drugs as I stowed her beneath the seat in front
of me, cradling her between my sandaled feet to protect
her from being crushed or harmed by turbulent skies.

She was a beautiful young sapling, the offspring of one

of the trees that grew in the back yard of my childhood home at 204. When we bought our little white house, our first task was to plant her firmly into the ground in a place where I could witness her beauty as she grew, worship her steadfastness, and write my stories within the grace and grasp of her tenacious spirit. I called her Marion after your grandmother. It seemed fitting.

The first day of school starts tomorrow. Those giggly-girl days of anticipation and preparation are far behind us now. No more shopping for new clothes, shoes, school supplies, backpacks and lipstick.

But this isn't about looking back but about the art of the possible. And that exists in today and tomorrow. Not yesterday.

First and foremost Girl Warrior Daughters, I want all big and beautiful, audacious and daring, large, large, large things for your life. I don't know what those are. But you do. Define your own largeness.

Don't merely chase after your dreams. Devour them. Like they were the best meal of your life. Your last supper. Your first taste of sugar. Your introductory slug of booze. Your biggest addiction. Slay them to the bone.

Then grind the bone to powder, put it in your shake, and swallow it good and hard. Drink it up.

Don't smooth out your rough edges. Unless you want to. Any refining that takes place should come at your hand, not that of another. But before you pull out the refiner's wheel take a long unfaltering look at those rough edges and be certain that you want to eradicate them, make them even and polished. Within the crevices, spikes and prickles are all the brilliant things that make you interesting. Not always "nice" or "easy" or "sweet" but so fucking interesting and fascinating and curious and so damned irresistible. So utterly breathtaking to me.

Take your time to figure it out, whatever "it" is. But remember that time as we know it, during this present earthly trip we call our life, is finite. Sad but true. While the possibilities might be infinite, your time to explore, employ, enact and enjoy all the prospects and promises is not. So don't waste or squander, throw away or spend this time recklessly pursuing things that don't really matter to you. Don't blow things off for tomorrow. Instead, do a little something of what you love every day. It doesn't have to be a big deal, just something that made getting out of bed worthwhile.

Don't worry about the good opinions of others. You are none of their business. What goes on inside your head and heart belongs to you, is sacrosanct, sacred and untouchable. Express yourself respectfully but freely and always from a place of personal truth. At times this will require courage, and those really big-girl pants, but it's imperative that you speak up when called to, break the silence when necessary, stand up for your convictions, and take a Girl Warrior stance. Do this regardless of who agrees or disagrees.

And last but most importantly Girl Warrior Daughters, know that you are always good enough.

And I love you dearly.

Your Girl Warrior Mama-Boo

ABOUT THE AUTHOR

Boo King is the founder of Girl Warrior Productions and is dedicated to working with women of all ages to visualize and create successful, inspired, powerful and authentic lives. She has spent the last twenty-five as a producer, copywriter, author, publisher, teacher, motivational speaker, bad musician and backdoor activist. She is the author of *Summer in a Red Mustang with Cookies*, a coming of age novel and *We Are The Girl Warriors*, an inspirational book of essays. And she loves dogs.

Boo King is available for select readings and speaking engagements. To inquire about a possible appearance, please contact Girl Warrior Productions at info@girlwarriorproductions.com.